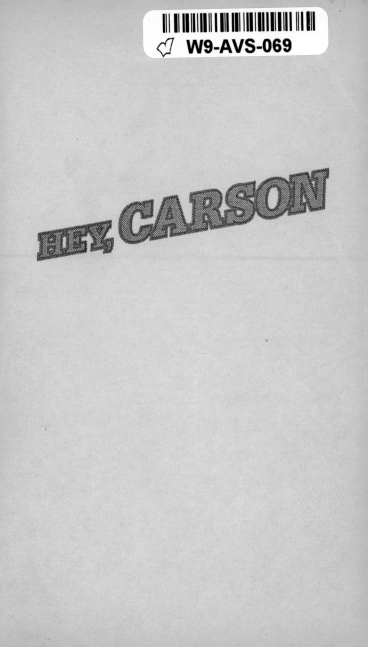

HEY, CARSON

HEY, CARSON

Meet
TRL's
Carson
Daly

By A. Pearl

SCHOLASTIC INC.

New York   Toronto   London   Auckland   Sydney
Mexico City   New Delhi   Hong Kong

This unofficial biography is not authorized by or affiliated with Carson Daly or the producers or stars of *TRL*.

ISBN 0-439-20759-2

12 11 10 9 8 7 6 5 4 3 2   0 1 2 3 4 5 6/0

Printed in the U.S.A.
First printing, July 2000   Scholastic

CHAPTER COUNTDOWN

CHAPTER 1 Hello Carson   1

CHAPTER 2 In the Beginning   4

CHAPTER 3 Voiceover   13

CHAPTER 4 We're Rolling   21

CHAPTER 5 Carson Moments   38

CHAPTER 6 Best Bud   47

CHAPTER 7 A New York Apartment   51

CHAPTER 8 Love Life   55

CHAPTER 9 Cool Carson Concepts   65

CHAPTER 10 Private Daly   72

CHAPTER 11 Fan Fair   82

CHAPTER 12 Total Trivia   91

CHAPTER 13 Get in Touch   101

HEY, CARSON

CHAPTER 1

Hello Carson

New York City, Manhattan.

It's a bitter, snowy day, but that doesn't stop the fans. Big blue barricades, resembling hands across America, are lined up on the street, preventing excited teens from entering into Times Square's busy street. Police patrol the area, trying to control the crowd.

This scene is a familiar one. And it happens every day. West Forty-fifth street is always packed with loyal, screaming teens. Some hold signs that say "We love you, Carson." "You're so sweet." "Will you marry me?" Others wave giant posters in the air, Carson's face plastered all over the posters. Many jump up and down, shrieking out his name, trying to get noticed by the hot hunk of MTV's most popular show, *TRL* — short for *Total Request Live.*

Carson Daly, unfazed and smiling, looks down from the huge signature second floor window onto the street. He waves to his adoring fans, who yell happily as they wave back. Even though the show doesn't go live for another hour, there are already more than one hundred people hanging outside. Some have been waiting all day.

Meet Carson Daly. The sweet, full-of-personality hottie who is the big draw of all this attention. Hard to believe that the guy with the cool charm and winning smile once toyed with the idea of becoming a professional golfer — *or* a priest! Harder to believe that just three years ago, he was a deejay in a small, almost unknown radio station in a small town in California. Who knew he would end up hosting today's hottest TV show? Not even Carson.

This is a story about a guy who cares deeply about his work, his family, and his fans. It's a story about a dream come true. And mostly, a story that couldn't happen to a nicer guy. So kick back and grab some of Carson's favorites snacks; Slim Jims, Otter Pops, and a Tombstone pizza, and read on. But buckle up. It's going to be a fast, fun ride on the fame train.

CHAPTER TWO
In the Beginning

Sunny Santa Monica, California, is home to the Daly family. Carson Jones Daly was born there on June 22, 1973. From the get-go, he was an easygoing, fun-loving, and adorable child.

His family included his mom Pattie, dad J.D., and older sister Quinn, who was three when Carson arrived.

When Carson was six years old, his dad, J.D., died of gallbladder cancer. As you can imagine, the Daly family was devastated and overcome with grief. This was an especially hard time for young Carson, but the adjustment was made easier a few years later when his mom married Richard Caruso, an entrepreneur — and all around great guy. It didn't take long for Carson and Richard to bond. The two became extremely close. In fact, Carson credits his stepdad for his own strong work ethic and morals.

His parents were open-minded but strict. Even with his passion for music, Carson wasn't allowed to go to any concerts until he was seventeen years old. Of course, he's since made up for his lack of concert attendance, having been to over five hundred events since he got into the music industry. Carson was an obedient kid. He never got in trouble or gave his mom a hard time. "My mom's motto," he told *Teen Magazine*, "was 'Nothing good happens after midnight,' and for a long time I actually believed it."

Carson attended Santa Monica High School in Southern California. Called "Samohi" by the students and faculty, the school is just a few blocks from the beach and ocean. Although *his* parents weren't mega-wealthy, Carson grew up surrounded by an exclusive group of celebrities and their kids. Chad Lowe (*Popular*) and his older brother Rob (*West Wing*) went to the same school as Carson. Actors Michelle Pfeiffer and Charlie Sheen lived nearby. He hung out with famous children like Jane Fonda's son, Troy, and musician Jackson Browne's son, Ethan. Stardom was all around him — but Carson was never starstruck. Although he didn't know it back then, that quality that would serve him well later on!

Hitting the Green

During his high school days, Carson's favorite activity was playing golf. Many of Carson's after school hours were spent on the green rather than hanging out with girls or partying. "I was a four-year varsity letterman in golf, which is like, the lamest sport," Carson told the *New York Daily News*. If you asked him what he wanted to be when he grew up, he would have said "a professional golfer." That is, until something happened to change his mind — something *very* powerful. It made him decide to become — not a TV star like he is now, but a Catholic priest.

Touched by a Feeling

When Carson was in his mid-teens, he was in Los Angeles eating lunch with a group of friends at a local hangout. Suddenly, out of nowhere, he felt something warm and comforting on his head. "It stayed there a good fifteen seconds. But when I looked around, no one was touching me!" he related in *Teen People* magazine. "Then I started having hot flashes. My eyes began to burn, and I started to sweat. My mind started racing — I thought about how lucky I was to live in California and to have such great friends and supportive parents. Then, unbelievably, my brain became awash with even bigger issues, like world poverty! All at once, I realized how much I had and how badly I wanted to use it to help others."

After the feeling passed, he raced over to the nearest pay phone and called his mom. He tried to explain what had happened to him, but he could tell that his mother thought he'd gone momentarily bonkers. All Carson could do was say he loved her, and that he wanted to thank her for everything she had ever done for him. Still, she wasn't getting it. So Carson relayed the whole story again, this time more slowly, trying to explain all his feelings. Finally, his mom started to understand. "I explained how, for the first time, I realized that I owed somebody something for my life and all of the good things in it; that we didn't just spontaneously appear on earth, but there are reasons for our lives," he continued to the *Teen People* reporter.

He wasn't as open with his friends as he was with his mom. At first, he figured, if his mom had a little trouble believing the story, his friends would be *totally* confused.

But Carson felt he had had a revelation and it was impossible to hide it from his buddies. His personality had changed. His outlook on life had been altered, too. Even what he thought of himself had taken a 180-degree turn. He started having a deeper relationship with his parents. He'd have really good talks with them, opening up and sharing more about himself and his goals. He wanted to hold onto his morals and clean-cut attitude. In short, Carson felt as though he had found God.

With all the changes that were happening, he couldn't keep his secret any longer. He decided to tell his friends — happily, they were totally cool with his revelation.

Because of his intensified belief, Carson was never tempted to do things like smoke cigarettes, or worse. Instead, he turned to his faith and strong religious beliefs in times of trouble. "I've trusted God and leaned on Him in tough times since my junior year in high school. My faith keeps my priorities in check," he told a reporter.

Carson has never pushed his beliefs on others. Rather, he just likes to let people know this is part of who he is. His love for a higher being is part of the big package.

During his senior year of high school, he attended Mass every day — at 6:00 AM! — "just to give thanks." Because of his religious beliefs, and the experience he went through, it was no surprise that Carson entered his senior year seriously considering becoming a Roman Catholic priest.

But he was torn. He was still passionate about golf and would hit the green each day. He was good, too. By age eighteen, he was ranked as one of California's top high-school golfers. He'd played with University of California-Los Angeles' golf team, hit several balls in the American Junior Golf Association, and even competed against Tiger Woods. When he graduated from high school at age nineteen, he couldn't put off making a decision about his future any longer.

Teed Off

Loyola Marymount University — his father's alma mater — offered him a scholarship to study and to play golf on their team. Carson accepted thinking he would study theology *and* play lots and lots of golf — combining his two passions. It sounded great — in theory.

Although Carson doesn't talk about it, things obviously didn't go as planned. After the first semester he dropped out. He applied to another college, this time in Palm Springs. By now he realized the priesthood probably wasn't for him, but a career as a professional golfer was still a possibility — for a while. But too much of a good thing and you can really burn out, and Carson did.

By the end of his sophomore year, Carson still didn't know what direction to head in. So he thought about another passion. He wasn't a singer, or a musician, but he loved being around music. And he was a great talker. A career as a deejay seemed like it could work. Carson had always been passionate about music and as a child had dreamed of working at a radio station. His first choice was working at one of the most influential radio stations in California, KROQ. "I'd even sit in front of the mirror and practice saying '106.7 KROQ,'" he told the *New York Post.*

Wanting to get into radio was one thing — *how* to do it was another. Carson didn't know the first thing about it. It was sheer coincidence that at the very same time Carson was in Palms Springs searching for a way in the door, his good friend Jimmy Kimmble was also there. As fate would have it, Jimmy was working as a deejay at a local radio station called KCMJ.

He suggested that Carson give it a try. Jimmy, who can now be seen on Comedy Central's *Win Ben Stein's Money* and *The Man Show*, got him an interview. Carson was on his way.

CHAPTER THREE
Voiceover

Following Jimmy's advice, Carson applied for an internship at KCMJ. His easygoing personality and eagerness helped him win the job. But there was a catch. When Carson accepted the position, he had no idea part of his responsibilities would involve being — no kidding — a *pheasant!* Carson, dressed from head to toe in feathers, would waddle onto the street. The idea, silly as it was, was to draw attention to the radio station. It worked. People pointed and honked at him. "At seven A.M., I'd have to go out to the busiest intersection in town, wearing a tutu or a chicken suit, and people would call in and win concert tickets for spotting what I was wearing," he confessed to *TV Guide*. But

Carson didn't mind the "unusual" dress code. He had a blast.

Carson relished the radio life and the whole music scene. "Being on the radio is like [the good part of] being grounded in your room," he said in an interview. It wasn't long before he was learning important rules of radio — and demonstrating the modesty he's become known for. "If you have an esophagus and a pulse," he told a reporter, "you, too, can be on the air."

But even though Carson loved his job, after a while he felt he needed more. That "more" was another job — in addition to the one he had. Carson headed to a different radio station. This one played alternative music. But there was a big drawback. The gig was in San Diego, about one hundred miles away from Palm Springs. Ouch! For six months, he woke up early, hit his first job at KCMJ, and then, after a grueling day, drove to job number two. Even though this made Carson beyond exhausted, it was well worth it. KCMJ gave him the opportunity to hone his personality and develop a radio style. Moonlighting at the radio station in San

Diego gave Carson an introduction to the kind of music he could really bond with.

Hard to believe, but even with his two jobs, Carson felt unfulfilled. So he decided to look for other opportunities. He moved in with his older sister, Quinn, who was living near San Francisco. He still wanted to stay in radio, and knew he would eventually find the perfect station as long as he kept looking. He got a part time job working at Live 105 FM in San Francisco, but the gig was short-lived. Even though he enjoyed the work, it quickly became routine for him. He wanted to be creative, play the music he liked, introduce the world to new bands and talent, and do interviews with famous musicians.

Carson's spirits were lifted when he snagged a job in 1995, doing the cool afternoon shift at KOME in San Jose, California. There, Carson found some enjoyment and was content for a while. But he soon got itchy again and looked for something else. By this time he'd already clocked *five* jobs in radio in a few short years. He was moving forward — just not fast enough.

Gradually, Carson had been working at bigger and more prominent radio stations. But the biggest break came when he snagged an audition at KROQ in Los Angeles. Vice President of Programming, Kevin Weatherly, was impressed by Carson's radio skills and charming personality. He was also impressed with Carson's sense of humor, his ability to connect with musicians, and to give a lot of information in few words — three really important attributes to have for radio. And thanks to all the moving around, he had developed a cool fan following.

Carson was twenty-three when KROQ gave him a shot. This was pretty monumental because the station hadn't hired someone full-time for seven years. Carson was in radio heaven.

At KROQ he was reunited with pal Jimmy, the man responsible for getting him a job in radio in the first place. Jimmy, too, had jumped from one radio station to another. Now they were together.

At KROQ Carson really came into himself. Not only was he given the prime time spot, six to ten P.M., but his creativity was encouraged. Carson took full advantage of that. He started hanging out with famous musicians — ordered Domino's pizza with U2 — went to parties and awards shows, and interviewed bands like Hole, Foo Fighters, and Bush. He also developed some signature habits — like painting his fingernails black. He even pierced his nose and wore punk rock T-shirts and went around saying: "That's cool," "That's not cool."

His first major assignment for KROQ was covering the 1995 MTV Video Music Awards live from New York City. At that event, he scored an interview with Alanis Morissette. Like Carson, she was trying to make a name for herself and get noticed. Carson didn't know it then, but he would be the first person in America to interview the unconventional, funky singer. This interview put Carson on the map.

Lots of people caught that radio show, including some executives from MTV.

I Want My MTV

A few days after the awards, a rep from MTV called asking the cute deejay if he would be interested in working with them. For Carson, this was the chance of a lifetime. "MTV was looking for guest VJs for the summer," Carson told *Newsday*. The show MTV had in mind was called *Beach House*. The job was for three months and would be shot in California. Even though MTV heard him interview Alanis, and liked Carson's voice, they needed a bit more convincing. MTV suggested Carson make a tape of himself introducing music videos to show his on-air capabilities.

Carson wasted no time taking MTV's advice and quickly put together an audition tape. He introduced some videos and kept his whole approach "real." One of the bands he introduced was No Doubt and played their song, "Don't Speak." Even though this was his first audition for tape, he was calm, cool, and collected. He just kept saying, "Be myself, they'll like me for me." And he was right.

MTV liked Carson's tape, a lot, and offered him the short-term job.

Life's a Beach

Beach House aired in May 1997. Not surprisingly, Carson took to the cameras as a fish takes to water. His smile and eyes drew in viewers, his charm won them over. In short, he was a natural. To Carson, this was a dream come true. Not only did he get to be involved in the music world, he got to interact with people, move around on different sets, and hang out on the beach. What could be better?

Things went so smoothly that MTV offered him another stint. This time he'd be a full-fledged "resident" on a show called *Motel California*.

Summer is usually a time for relaxing and taking a break, kicking back and catching some rays. Not for Carson. His face popped up everywhere that summer on MTV. He hosted, told jokes, did some reporting, and had a blast. He did fashion segments, asked the question of the day, interviewed celebrities, and chatted with other MTV hosts. Then MTV asked him to introduce some upcoming events, and even show off his great tan. Carson wasn't just working the beach scene, he was owning it.

Like *Beach House, Motel California* was a short-lived show. And when the summer was over, Carson assumed he would go back to radio. MTV, however, had other plans for him. The network offered Carson the opportunity to work on another project. This one was would be taped live.

CHAPTER FOUR
We're
Rolling

It was called *MTV Live*, and the concept was simple: the host had to look cute, ask the question of the day, screen some callers, interview hot musicians such as K-Ci and Busta Rhymes, premiere a video or two, and chat with "surprise" guests. What you see is what you get — mistakes, surprises, and all. *MTV Live* set up shop between West 44th and 45th streets, and used the real life New York City for a backdrop.

Carson accepted the gig immediately, even though it meant moving to New York with little more than just a suitcase. He was cool with it. *MTV Live* wasn't *too* big a change for him since he had been doing live radio. "In my opinion," he told a reporter, "there's very little difference. For one thing, there's the live element. When I said something into that mike, it went right out onto the air. It's the same with MTV, only with a camera."

Carson actually loved the live aspect. He enjoyed knowing he was living in the moment, that anything could happen. The fans felt the same way. And each night at six P.M., viewers would gather around West 45th Street to watch and be part of the whole experience.

What's in a Name?

In 1998, MTV also had a show called *Total Request*. It presented a video countdown, and had revolving hosts. It wasn't making the grade in the ratings. Unfortunately, Carson's show, *MTV Live*, wasn't doing too well either. Even though the talent was great and kids were into it, the numbers that make a show a hit just weren't there. Rather than cancel both shows, MTV decided to combine them by taking the live element and adding it to the countdown. It was the perfect solution.

The new version was called *Total*

Request Live. Its predecessors *MTV Live* and *Total Request* had been hour-long shows but MTV tacked on an additional half hour to the hybrid to introduce world premiere videos and have longer visits by celebrities. MTV also decided to have just one host for *Total Request Live.* That person, of course, was Carson. Almost automatically, ratings went through the roof.

By March 1999, *Total Request Live* got so popular, MTV began referring to it by its initials — *TRL.* Easier to say, easier to like. *TRL* counted down the top ten videos, invited kids from the street to come into the studio audience, scrolled e-mails across the screen, and chatted with fans and celeb guests. There were call-ins from famous musicians, exclusive interviews, and world premiere videos.

Eventually the show went back to being on for one hour. To compensate and not lose quality time with guests, *TRL* viewed only *part* of some videos rather then play all of them in their entirety. Fan input and comments were heard over the video as well. To keep things moving and interesting, MTV decided that after a particular video is on the countdown sixty-five times, it's retired to the big vault in the sky, no matter how popular it remains.

"Welcome to the Show"

TRL had finally found its niche, its spot, and its name. And West 45th Street became "Teen Central," an after school hangout where friends hooked up and hung out. Those who were strangers in the beginning bonded by the one thing they had in common, their love and admiration for Carson. Part of what made *TRL* a huge melting pot was the diverse music the show played. "I like to call it the United Nations of music-video shows," Carson explained to the *New York Post*. "Everybody gets represented." It's probably the only place you'll ever see the Backstreet Boys mixing with Nine Inch Nails and Smash Mouth.

Carson feels the music has also diversified. "There's a lot more crossover now, whether it's rock bands using dance beats or rappers sampling guitars." Carson's not the only one who sees change happening. "Young fans are hungry for variety," Tom Calderone, MTV's Senior Vice

President of Music and Talent told *Alternative Press.* "I don't think five years ago you could have had Stone Temple Pilots and Coolio on the same show and have it work. Now you can have Jay-Z and Limp Bizkit on the same show and it does work." But in an ideal Carson world, boy bands would get along with the rockers, the heavy metalists would hold hands with the rappers, and Britney Spears and Puff Daddy would lock arms and shop together.

Today, the show reflects what's hot and what's not. *TRL* has become a driving force in the music industry — you want it, they play it. The shows had everyone on from Marc Anthony to 'N Sync. From Beck to Foo Fighters. In between have been Christina Aguilera, Britney Spears, Brandy, Lenny Kravitz, Mariah Carey, Will Smith, Backstreet Boys, Jewel, Kid Rock, Limp Bizkit, Smash Mouth, Rage Against the Machine . . . the list is endless. Actors, too, find their way to the stage. Bill Murray, Freddie Prinze, Jr., Melissa Joan Hart, Mike Myers, Natalie Portman, and Jennifer Love Hewitt have all appeared on the show too. And that's just a sampling.

TRL also gives away great goodies.

Everyday *TRL* raffles away T-shirts, notebooks, and concert tickets. In between video clips and celebrity interviews Carson smiles and waves, talks and makes funny jokes. Carson has told his fans that working at MTV is a small step away from working at Disneyland. No lines, no waiting, and you get the royal treatment. There's also lots of food, plus fun perks like concert tickets, clothing, and cool people. And let's not forget, it's fun to watch and each show is different every day. "The best part for me is putting the least likely people in the same room," Carson told the *New York Post*. "One show we had the Wu-Tang Clan and Britney Spears and Melissa Joan Hart. I'm standing in the middle of them all and Wu-Tang's like, 'Whassup girl?'"

Today, *TRL* is one of MTV's highest rated shows, watched by more than a million viewers a day. *Newsweek* called *TRL* a "not to be missed New York event."

How It Works

What helps make *TRL* such a huge success? The viewers! Since it's a viewer requested show, teens have a lot of power.

They call in or e-mail MTV requesting their favorite video. The numbers are then tallied up and presto — you've got *TRL*'s top ten for the next day. MTV's lines are open 24/7 and are the direct link to what kids want to see and hear.

No tickets are needed to see the show but fans do have to be eighteen or older to get into the studio audience. Sixty to eighty lucky people are picked daily by the MTV talent department (at random from the kids on West 45th Street) to be on the show. Carson has a little pull too, and he can point or spot someone he'd like to join the audience while a video is playing. E-mails and phone-in messages run along the bottom of the screen. Fans who are still outside often introduce videos or are shown squealing and cheering for their request.

Carson announces when certain guests or bands will be on so fans can make sure to come down and catch their favorites. Today, *TRL* is such a hot and exciting attraction, teens and their parents fly in from all over the world just to sneak a peek and watch the scene from the street.

How It Looks

Many of the lucky who have graced the inner sanctum of MTV's *TRL* set have said the studio is much smaller than they thought. There are two large boards where all the celebrity guests have left autographs. The decor and design of MTV is cool. Gold and platinum records cover the walls like wallpaper. There are pictures of famous singers and celebrities in large frames. MTV even has a reception desk that looks like a huge boulder with a person sitting beside it. TVs are everywhere.

Changes?

From the beginning, Carson thought of himself as the link between the fans and the videos. Kids request what they want to see, and who should be in what spot, and Carson would deliver the information. He was very aware that *TRL* was not called, *The Carson Daly Show.* "The show is not about me or my tastes. If I had my way [with the videos and guests], it would probably surprise a lot of people," Carson said during MTV's on-line chat. "The beauty of the show is that MTV gives you ninety minutes every day to pick the videos. I just play them and get a chuckle out of the Korn fans fighting against the Backstreet fans for the number-one spot. *TRL* is a rare home for everybody."

Translation: Carson *doesn't* get to play what *he* likes. "If you think I like everything I present, you're crazy," he admitted to *YM*. If he did, you could bet there'd be some pretty big changes. Maybe he'd play more Korn and less Backstreet Boys or boot Britney and Mandy for the Beastie Boys. Who knows? Carson isn't saying exactly.

Band-Aid

TRL is more than just a great show. It's responsible for far more than creating a little musical harmony. It's helped make some bands household names. "Limp Bizkit had been around for a number of years," said MTV News' head Dave Sirulnick, who helped make *TRL* a reality. "Then the masses started voting for them on *TRL* and before you knew it, Fred Durst became a certified rock star." Carson and

TRL have helped groups like Smash Mouth make it big. The band thanked Carson personally in front of millions of viewers at the MTV Video Awards when they accepted their trophy. And don't forget about Britney Spears. Before *TRL*, many people didn't know who she was. When Carson played her video, ". . . Baby One More Time," for the first time, her popularity skyrocketed. The next day, tons of teens requested the video and it hit number one within a week. Barry Weiss, President of Jive Records, agreed that *TRL* has had a major impact on the popularity of his artists. On Friday, Dec. 11, 1998, he was in a meeting, giving a presentation, "and in the middle of it, at one o'clock, we got news that Britney's '. . . Baby One More Time' video had made it on the *TRL* countdown at number ten," he recalled. That's when he knew Britney would be a success. And you can't forget Jordan Knight, one-time New Kid on the Block-er. He credits the show with helping to launch his solo career last April. "Just off of *TRL*, my single grew," he told a reporter. That song was "Give It to You," which hit the *Billboard* charts.

The Host With the Most

Carson is a great interviewer. That's no secret. He's able to talk to anyone and to pick up on their mood and personality. "If Christina Aguilera is on the show, I just ask her how her life has changed, how school has changed, what her friends think of her fame," Carson shared with a reporter. "If it's Zack de la Rocha from Rage, it's a totally different vibe." Knowing how to talk to people is one of Carson's best qualities. His mother thinks this talent came from growing up in LA and hanging out with famous folks. Surrounded by the famous and the rich, Carson felt comfortable and at ease. "I think one reason Carson interviews celebrities so well is because we'd go to the market, and there they were," Pattie told *TV Guide*.

His mom is not alone in her thinking. Many others agree that Carson's real talent is his laid back, make-you-feel-at-home attitude. "You could have the most hard-core guests on the show," David Saslow, head of Interscope Records Video Promotion Department, told *Teen Celebrity*, "and he finds a way to make them feel comfortable."

The stars themselves weigh in on Carson — and *TRL*'s influence. "While I was recording 'Genie in a Bottle,'" Christina Aguilera admitted to *TV Guide*, "I used to watch *TRL* before I went to the studio."

"It makes you want to make a better video, or beat out the person who spent a million dollars on their video," Kid Rock said in the same article. "Carson's got crazy personality," 'N Sync-er Justin Timberlake, told *USA Today*. "I think that if MTV ever made the mistake of letting him go, he could have his own sitcom, man." Would he? Well, he *has* been writing a lot lately. He's got a ton of sitcom and movie ideas rolling around in a head already filled to the brim with music trivia, facts and information.

Nervous?

Some people get antsy before a live show. Others freak out. Some even get sick. Carson is like a rock. He may get a little jumpy, but he never gets so scared that he doesn't want to go on. "My mom told me, 'If you don't get nervous, you're not doing a good job,'" Carson said in *Newsday*. "I'm always a little bit nervous but I've done so much live work in two years, I'm pretty used to it now. I could care less about celebrity status," he told a fan on MTV Chat. "I get nervous cause I'm about to go on national TV and people have the assumption that I am one hundred percent prepared, confident, and know exactly what I'm doing. When in reality, [sometimes] I don't. When the camera goes on, I just pretend like I'm talking to a room full of my friends."

What to Wear?

When Carson was doing radio, he used to just show up, wearing whatever he wanted. A wake-up-and-roll-out-of-bed look can be very appealing on some people. Carson is one of them. "You wear anything you want and play loud music," he told a reporter. "My grandfather was a mens wear retailer in Los Angeles. The first thing I learned about fashion was how to hang pants." Not an important tip for radio, since no one can see you, but a good bit of knowledge for TV.

Carson is not vain. He couldn't care less if his hair isn't perfectly coifed. And he doesn't love being fussed over by the makeup artists, hair people, or clothing designers who work on his image. "When I'm in makeup," he confessed to *Seventeen*, "I'm like, 'Am I done yet?'" Very often Carson will show up totally unshaven. He wants fans to see him as his true self — even if that sometimes means messy hair and pizza stained clothing! Carson would love to wear an old pair of jeans and a T-shirt with a band's insignia scribbled on it to work every day.

No Pushover

Carson is the king of nice, but that doesn't mean he's a pushover. On the contrary. His high morals and good values make him a guy who stands his ground.

One time MTV wanted him to ask the audience a question he didn't feel comfortable asking. Carson found it inappropriate. He stood his ground as he has so many times before, and suggested something more age appropriate. Carson won the battle and went on to ask his audience members a broader, not so personal question.

Hard Work?

Work? Carson thinks of his job as play. He's having a great time chatting with music celebs and helping fans' dreams come true. "I feel like I'm in my living room, and all these cool people who just happen to be famous drop by to hang out," Carson admitted to *USA Today*. "I'm nothing more than the Willy Wonka of MTV. I just take the kids into the Wonka factory and open the gates to their wildest dreams." Another perk? He is a man with connections. If he needs to get concert tickets for a friend or relative, he just calls the musicians directly on their cell phones or pagers. That means Carson is also a man with lots of numbers.

Of course, there *is* a downside. Sometimes it is hard to be "on" all the time, and to keep up his energy. He has to do it every day of his life whether he feels good, or not. Happy, sad, tired, bored, whatever, he has to show up. Just like everyone else, Carson has good days and bad days. "I have people in my life who get sick, and *I* get sick, and I have to go out and talk about music and go out with a smile, and it gets hard sometimes," he confessed during an on-line chat. "[But] it's also the best part about the job because if people aren't feeling good they can turn you on [TV] and you can make them feel good. It works both ways."

The most difficult part, perhaps, is receiving bad news and knowing that you've still got to go out there and smile. When Carson found out his mother had been diagnosed with breast cancer, he had to be on the set in twenty minutes. He didn't have time to deal or recover from the blow. He had to be in front of the camera and put on a good act. No wonder he sometimes feels when the camera light goes on he *is* sort of acting.

Perfection

Carson is a perfect mix. He's funny without being corny. He's sarcastic without being mean. He's really smart, but doesn't come off as a know-it-all. He's kind without being a wimp. He's good looking without being too pretty. And his fans love him, his parents are crazy about him, his co-workers enjoy being with him, no one has a bad thing to say about this guy. And it's all true. He's gotten so much buzz and become so popular, there's no telling what Carson's next move will be. The world is his.

CHAPTER FIVE
Carson
Moments

Though Carson doesn't have a true favorite — at least not one he can admit to — he does have songs that make his personal list. His criteria? "Any time a song can change your outlook on life, you know it's a great song."

Here's a list of artists you'd probably find in Carson's CD collection.

Kid Rock	Devil Without a Cause	"Only God Knows Why"
Pennywise	About Time	"Perfect People"
Rage Against the Machine	Rage Against the Machine	"Know Your Enemy"
Black Metallic	Ferment Catherine	"Wheel"
Beastie Boys	Paul's Boutique	"Hey Ladies"
Nine Inch Nails	Fisted Box	"March of the Pigs"
No Doubt	Tragic Kingdom	"Spiderwebs"
Third Eye Blind	Third Eye Blind	"Jumper"
Blink 182	Enema of the State	"What's My Name Again"

Oops!

The world is an imperfect place and the set of *TRL* is no different. Even though mostly it's smooth sailing, there have been a few surprise goof-ups along the way. Here are a few of the funny, unexpected bloopers.

1. Wake-up Call: Actor Pierce Brosnan needed a little shut eye — and chose to take his winks on the air. "He kept falling asleep," Carson told *Twist.*

2. We're Rolling: Once Carson didn't realize the cameras were on. And since the show is live, an unprepared Carson was chit chatting away, making jokes and goofing around. Carson stayed grounded and cool.

3. Fright Fight: One time the Foo Fighters were guests on the show. The other guests were professional Wrestlers Diamond Dallas Page and The Raven. The mix was not a good one — the two groups got into a real fight while the cameras were rolling. That's not very good guest behavior.

4. Clipped: While interviewing funny man Al Franken, a clip was rolled too early. Quick thinking, always unflappable Carson jokingly said, "Hey, stop that clip." He yukked it up with Al all on live TV and waited for the correct and scheduled time for the clip to play. Close call. Carson to the rescue!

Cool People

Carson loves to interview film and TV celebrities almost as much as he enjoys talking to the musicians — in fact, he's even more relaxed with actors. "I don't feel like I was hired to interview them," Carson shared with MTV Chat, "so if I messed it up, who could get mad?" He also enjoys introducing bands who got started around the same time he did. "Bands that I've known before I worked at MTV who finally made it are my favorites," he told fans during an on-line chat. "It's like all the dorks at a party who couldn't get in, and then the doors open and we could *all* run in at the same time and indulge." That list includes Smash Mouth, No Doubt, Blink 182, and Third Eye Blind.

Carson has made some tight, long lasting friendships with many people he's interviewed. Here are three of his most memorable guests.

1. President Bill Clinton. "I met the President, that was exciting," Carson told Jay Leno back in 1999 on *The Tonight Show*. "He gave a speech and I was there. Then he came down the [receiving] line and I thought, 'This is my moment with the President. I'm going to say something to him that no one has ever said to him.'" But all Carson could think to say was, "So . . . how's everything going?" Even though that wasn't original, the President didn't seem to mind. In fact, he was really nice and gave Carson a moment to figure out what he wanted to ask. This time Carson was on the other end of the interview and was momentarily speechless.

2. Marilyn Manson: Carson, a little nervous about interviewing the controversial performer, followed his own rule of thumb: be prepared. "I read everything on him. I thought, 'I'm going to know more about this guy than he knows about himself, and

that way he's going to respect me and it'll be cool.'" The two met in the makeup room first. There, Marilyn asked Carson's opinion of his rings. Carson's reaction? *"This* is what I was worried about?" Of course there was no need to fear. The interview went great and the two have become friends. Plus, Carson says Marilyn's one of the smartest people he's ever met.

3. Hanson: Carson liked these three brothers not only for their talent, but because they broke the mold. At first, no one thought the band would be successful. But Hanson proved everyone wrong. They attracted more people to *TRL* than his makeup-caked friend Marilyn, *or* 'N Sync *or* the Backstreet Boys!

Extra-Curricular Activities

Carson is more than just the host for *TRL,* he's become something of a Master of Ceremonies for MTV. In fact, MTV recently flew him out to LA to premiere the network's one-millionth video and *TRL's* new roadtrip across the country show.

He's also made guest appearances on numerous other MTV shows and special events like *Say What Karaoke*, *MTV Spring Break*, *Cool Crap Weekend*, *WWF Week*, *Snowed In*, and *Wannabe a VJ Too Search.*

This year Jesse Camp (who won the VJ title the year before), and Carson were on a mission to find the perfect VJ. Over two thousand people camped outside MTV's studios hoping to get the chance to audition for the prize of the host. Hosting is a hard title to fill. Carson knows this better than anyone else. Luckily, he was full of helpful tips. "What we're really looking for," he said to a reporter, "is somebody who's natural." Carson was Mr. Relaxed during *his* audition tape, and that really helped him secure his job at MTV. Each contestant had to read a script, introduce a video or two and talk a little bit about him or herself. Carson reminded viewers that MTV was not looking for an actor. "I would say, don't try and imitate anybody you've seen on MTV before. And show them that you know about music, you know, from rap to alternative." Good suggestion. Along with Jesse, MTV's Matt Pinfield, and former New Kid Joey McIntyre, Carson selected the five finalists and awarded the job to Laura Lifschitz. Lucky girl.

A Needed Break

Carson hardly gets any time off, and the turn of the century was no major exception. In preparation to host MTV's big millennium bash, Carson went home to California for three days during Christmas to be with his family and friends. But he barely had a chance to rest up before leaving. He flew back to New York to host the biggest countdown of the century. There he was in Times Square with over two million people screaming and yelling — saying good-bye to the twentieth century and hello to the twenty-first. The evening was beyond memorable. Over ten bands performed and lots of celebrities made appearances. Carson, of course, was the main attraction for most.

And who could forget MTV's Super Bowl Sunday party? Carson hosted a one hour *TRL* Super Bowl 2000 special. Lots of famous football players joined in on the games and festivities while 'N Sync sang some songs and got the crowd roaring with excitement. The show was taped live from the NFL Experience in Atlanta, Georgia. Carson delivered the ten most requested videos of the week with help from his co-host, *Dawson's Creek* star James Van Der Beek. It was one heck of a good time and Carson loved every minute of it.

Additionally, Carson has hosted *The Miss Teen USA* beauty pageant *and The 49th Miss USA Pageant*, and done live reports for TV's *Entertainment Tonight.*

Carson is also starring in commercials for Pizza Hut and CD.com — his face can be seen on almost any channel.

Sure, *TRL* and all his extra-curricular activities soak up a lot of Carson's time, but that doesn't stop the charismatic host from lending a hand at several worthy charities to benefit others. Carson has knocked a few pins over for the NBA First Annual Celebrity Bowling Party, shot hoops in Atlanta, Georgia's, State University Charity Event, and bounced some tennis balls around at the Arthur Ashe Kids'

Day. There Carson's job was to warm up 20,000 people who had shown up for the fourth annual event at the USTA National Tennis Center. Britney Spears also made a guest appearance and admitted she wasn't very good at tennis, so she sang instead! Carson even made a surprise appearance at a sixth grader's party at the All Star Cafe. Everyone was thrilled.

CHAPTER SIX
Best
Bud

They share a love of sports, work in the same place for the same company, and even live at the same address. Twenty-five-year-old Jason Ryan, one of MTV's hottest producers, wins the best bud award hands down.

Like Carson, Jason gave some serious consideration to becoming a professional athlete. Growing up, his dream was to be a famous baseball player, but eventually he realized the field wasn't his strongest suit. And like Carson, he fell into his line of work. In fact, producing for MTV was the farthest thing from his mind. "Five years ago, when I was sitting in my dorm room or my frat room," he admitted to a reporter, "never in my wildest dreams did I think I would be doing what I'm doing today." Jason thought he'd work in his hometown, Plainfield, Illinois, maybe do something in the financial or business world since that's what he was studying. Jason was in the middle of getting a degree in business when out of the blue he decided to hit the road, dissatisfied with college and not ready to do the 9-5 grind. He was only a credit and a half short of graduating. This was a huge risk and a life altering decision for Jason. Optimistic, he took a bus to New York. When he got out at the Port Authority bus terminal in Manhattan, he was petrified. There he was, in a strange place and didn't know a soul. He said, "New York is an intimidating city when you're out of college from Illinois."

At first, Jason thought he had made a terrible mistake. Perhaps he should go back home. But he didn't. Instead he took a deep breath and stayed in Manhattan for the night. One night turned into two. Two nights turned into one month, and one month became a year. Within that year, Jason worked at a variety of jobs. He ended up behind the scenes at MTV.

A hottie who's hip, but also humble —
that's the secret to *TRL*'s Carson

Taking a spin in *TRL*'s booth with fellow VJ, Ananda Lewis.

The view from here:
It is so not lonely at the top!

In happier times, Carson squired Jennifer Love Hewitt. They broke up in 1999

Carson's kitty is a cutie — just like him.

The cream of the rock, pop, Latin, metal, alt, and hip-hop crop bow at the altar of *TRL*. Getting on the show gives celebs instant star-cred. Just ask Britney (top) and ultra-cool country crooner LeAnn Rimes (bottom).

Carson's totally a "for-a-cause" boy: this benefit appearance was at the annual Arthur Ashe Kids' Day event in Flushing, New York.

Carson Daly

It's at this point in the story where Carson and Jason meet. Carson was hired to host *Beach House*, a project Jason was producing. "The first day I met him," Jason told *The Pantagraph*, a newspaper based in Bloomington, Illinois, "I knew he would become MTV's hottest property." And Jason was right.

From the get-go, they were instant friends. Each laughed at the other's jokes, each enjoyed going out after work. Carson's best quality, Jason told a reporter, was his loyalty, "like the friends I had in high school and in college. We're totally loyal to each other." In fact when the pals weren't hanging out together in Los Angeles, they were flying off to Las Vegas for a little rest and relaxation.

Now a year later, Jason is one of MTV's top talents. He has produced *The Real World*, *MTV's Music and Sports Festival*, and produced and directed Tori Amos' MTV special. As for Carson and Jason's relationship, the two are beyond tight. On any given day, they spend twelve to sixteen hours together.

Quick Bio:
Name: Jason Ryan
Hometown: Plainfield, Illinois
College: Graduated Fordham University in 1995
Birthday: October 3, 1973
Sign: Scorpio
Family: Dad, Roy; Mom, Loretta; brothers, Jonathan, 22 and Joshua, 18
Favorite Color: Blue
Favorite Bands: Blink 182, Filter, Limp Bizkit, Kid Rock, Smash Mouth
Favorite Movies: *The Game, Seven, Braveheart, Bull Durham, Field of Dreams*
Favorite Actors: Brad Pitt, Robert DeNiro, Harrison Ford

CHAPTER SEVEN
A New York Apartment

Like his pal Jason, Carson's transition to living in New York was not an easy one. Carson is so close to his family — especially his mom — that the move was really hard on him emotionally. Leaving warm, sunny California and all the comforts of home to relocate was tough. "I grew up on the beach in Santa Monica and all of a sudden I move to New York and have to find and apartment," Carson told Jay Leno. "You ask anybody 'Hey, where should I live, you know, I'm young,' and the camera guy says, 'Hey you should live on the Lower East Side, that's where all the bands play,' and, 'You should live downtown. *That's* where all the bands play,' so everybody is loyal to an area."

A big help was deciding to become roommates with Jason. The pair looked at several apartments all over the city, downtown in the Village, in the Lower East Side, the Lower West Side, even in hip Soho before settling on the chic Upper West Side.

Not big spenders, Carson and Jason didn't want to invest their paychecks in furniture. They've said that they use a broken oven as a file cabinet and for several months, the hunky host was sleeping on a big pile of his clothing. Ouch, not a comfy thought.

With Carson's busy schedule, you can bet he doesn't have time to bake, let alone have a "four-food-group" meal. Instead, he makes grilled cheeses from a Snackmaster. You might have seen him demonstrate when he was on *The Regis & Kathie Lee Show* — Chef Daly cooked up a real sandwich right there!

Carson's also a huge pizza fan. One time Carson and Jason went scouting for the perfect pizza. "We went to four markets looking for this stupid pizza. This is what consumes our lives on weekends," Carson admitted to *YM*. "I was like, 'You better hope this is the best pizza I've ever had.'"

Carson is a great host on TV, but when it comes to being a host in his own home, that's a whole other story. Before you bite into that grilled sandwich, you'd better make sure there aren't any surprises. "When people I don't like come over, I go for the anchovies. 'Cause you can stuff them in there and they'd never know," he shared with Regis and Kathie Lee.

The apartment includes a huge entertainment system and cherished golf video game. The walls are decorated with rock paraphernalia.

Carson and Jason are into staying home and renting lots of videos. They love DVD movies and favorites include: *Goodfellas*, *Donnie Brasco*, and *The Shawshank Redemption*.

When homesickness sets in, and Carson longs for the beach, the salt air, palm trees and warm sunny weather, he watches *Baywatch*. And of course, he calls his other best friend, his mom.

When Jason and Carson aren't working, the two can be found playing Golden-Tee, a video golf game at their neighborhood hangout, or just wandering down unknown streets in the city. Sometimes they hang out with their posse of famous musicians like, Kid Rock, 'N Sync, and Limp Bizkit. As long as Carson and Jason are together, they don't really care what they do. One of the best things about their friendship, Carson told *YM* is that "no matter how close you are to a girl, you still mind your own p's and q's. If I'm in a bad mood, it never affects us. With girls, there's peaks and valleys."

Their friendship is really 50/50. No one gives more than the other and no one is the taker. They help each other in every single aspect of their lives — especially in the love life department. "He helps me be more assertive because I'm terrified of women," Carson admitted to *YM*. "And he might be a little abrasive when he meets somebody, so I'll pull him aside and say, "'Dude, don't crack jokes about her hair! You like her!'"

Is there a down side to living with Carson? Just one. Jason says Carson loses his keys all the time.

CHAPTER EIGHT
Love
Life

It's no secret that family comes first with Carson. He's made that very clear in all his interviews and during his TV appearances. Carson and his mom have an unusually close relationship. She is truly his biggest fan. Pattie has always been hyper-supportive of her son and the decisions he's made.

These days, Pattie is almost as famous as Carson. She's been on MTV's *12 Angry Mothers*, phoned in during *TRL*, and has popped in to a few of her son's photo shoots. Recently, Pattie got a job following in her son's footsteps — as a talk-show host at a local cable show in Palm Springs, California.

Their tight bond may come from being through a lot together. Dad, J.D.'s, death was a real blow. Then, two years ago, more terrible news hit home. Pattie was diagnosed with breast cancer. Even though these were traumatic times, some good did come out of the situations. One, Pattie now has a clean bill of health, and two, Carson learned how fragile life can be and how lucky he is to have such a wonderful mom. On MTV's *12 Angry Mothers* Carson delivered the following message to his mom: "It's my turn to give a special Mother's Day message to my mom, one of the greatest women who ever stepped foot on the planet Earth. Mom, if you're out there, I hope you had the greatest Mother's Day ever. I love you very much. Happy Mother's Day."

Mothers sometimes tell embarrassing stories. Once Pattie shared a "Carsy Cakes" story when she was a guest on *MTV's 12 Angry Moms*. "She was sitting next to Puff Daddy's mom, and Busta Rhymes' mom," Carson recalled to *Teen*, "telling them about me running around as a little kid, pulling my pants down and stuff like that. I ran into Puffy later, and he wouldn't stop teasing me!"

Everyday Hero

Instead of looking up to celebrities for inspiration, Carson found that in his stepdad. "He got up early to go to work and came home late at night and never complained. As you get older you realize *that* is something to idolize," he told an interviewer. Now that Carson's able to pay his own way, he realizes how expensive things are. "My dad is definitely a hero." If Carson wasn't hosting *TRL*, he'd be working with his stepdad, who owns a golf shop. Richard was even Carson's "prom date." Because he didn't have a girl to go with, he and his stepdad watched TV all night. Not the most festive way to spend the prom evening, but Carson didn't mind. Neither did Richard.

Dating Dysfunction

Carson says he wasn't popular with the girls in school. But that didn't stop him from puckering up. He snagged his first kiss in the fourth grade. It was delivered on the playground to one of his classmates. After that, Carson says he had a dry spell for several years. Golfers weren't exactly chick magnets back then. "No girls wanted to go out with a guy on the golf team," he told *Twist.*

Carson's a great guy. He's open and sensitive, shy and sweet. The girls in his high school may not have liked him romantically, but they loved him as a person. His female classmates were always telling him they were so happy he was their friend rather than a boyfriend.

Carson attributes his lack of dating experience and his hard time finding Ms. Right because it's hard to live up to the women already in his life. His mom and sister, Quinn, are the best women he knows, and every time he meets a girl, he compares her to them. That can be a really tall order to fill.

Carson has also confessed to getting nervous on dates, so it's not surprising he's most attracted to someone who's humble, laid back, and not into fame. He wants someone to like him for him, instead of for his job. He's also really, really shy. He doesn't seem that way on TV, but it's true. He'd much prefer someone approach him and ask him out on a date. "Girls assume that, 'Well if he liked me, he'd come over here.' That's not true," he explained to *Twist*. "You should go over to me if you want to."

His ideal date? "To go someplace quiet, where you can hear each other," he described to the *New York Daily News*. "Where and what you're doing doesn't matter as long as you have a chance to talk and get to know each other."

Love to Love Ya

Carson had no idea that when a certain actress guested on *TRL* he would end up head over heels in love — or *with* Love.

He interviewed Jennifer Love Hewitt in the beginning of 1998. She stopped by the show to help promote *Teen People*'s first issue: she was the cover girl. Though it wasn't love at first sight, there was an instant chemistry. However, they didn't start dating until a year or so later. "The last time that I went on his show," Jennifer — called Love by her friends — shared with *Cosmopolitan* magazine, "we became friends and started talking on the phone."

Their official first date came when Carson went to visit his old stomping grounds in Los Angeles. He had a few days off and decided to head home. Love was working on *Party of Five* when Carson came to town. They got together for a date and enjoyed each other's company so much, they ended up spending the rest of Carson's time there together. "He's an amazing person," Love confessed to *Cosmo*. "Funny, incredibly smart, and so normal for somebody who does what he does. He's just a great human being." In *People* magazine she gushed, "His eyes are incredibly truthful — you can get lost in them. And he's down to earth."

Carson felt exactly the same way about Love. He saw how similar they were. They shared the same values, same ideas, and same traditional thinking. Carson thought he had found his soul mate. "She was the most humble, soft spoken, gracious person I'd ever met," he told *People*. He's also said that she's one of the hardest working people he knows, and one of the nicest. Carson was smitten.

Fan reaction to the high profile couple was mixed. Some were bummed — because it meant their hot host was no longer "available." Others were happy because Love was so well liked by everyone.

Since Love was also a celebrity, she understood the lifestyle and was unaffected by Carson's job, his fame, or his fans. He admitted to a reporter, "She looks at the screaming girls outside [his MTV window] and says, 'That's awesome, they're supporting the show' — and I look at her screaming guy fans as flattering."

Though there were more than three thousand miles between Carson in New York and Love in California, the distance didn't hurt the relationship. "We have a really good friendship," she told *Teen People*. "At this point it's quality, not quantity — which I think is better anyway." They went back and forth between the coasts, each sharing the travel responsibility. They e-mailed and spent an enormous amount of time on the phone. To compensate for their long distance relationship, the two talked four or more times a day. Can you say expensive long distance phone bill? Carson can.

They were still an item on Valentine's Day, 1999. When a reporter asked what Jennifer's V-day wish was, her answer was simple. "Just to be in the same state. That would be nice." Carson agreed, adding, he was in the best relationship he could ever have imagined. "I've never been happier." It seemed as though the two were inseparable even with the time difference and the large amount of land that came between them.

Before this relationship, being a celebrity never really mattered to Carson, nor had he felt it an imposition. But because both love birds were in the public eye, fame did take a toll on their relationship. Dining out was hard. People would stop and stare at the happy couple, who only wanted to be alone and make the most out of the short time they had to be together. Going to the movies was close to impossible, as was shopping, walking around a mall, even waiting in airports. Fans wanted photos or autographs. "Before we were dating, I used to think, 'Hey man, you're a public figure. You asked for it.' But now I understand how hard it is to have a private life," Carson confided to *Teen*.

Still their celebrity status didn't stop them from going out, or being seen in public. Carson and Love went to several award and movie premieres together like *MTV's Music Video Awards* and *I Still Know What You Did Last Summer*. Photos show the couple hand in hand smiling at each other and looking very lovey-dovey. The two also co-hosted *MTV's New Year's Eve Live 1998* where Method Man, Green Day, and Limp Bizkit performed. Much of the world saw sparks fly — not only in the sky, but in Carson's and Jennifer's eyes.

Because their pairing was so public, their October 1999 breakup came as a surprise to fans and to friends. They'd been together eighteen months. Only the two of them know for sure what caused the rift — and neither is commenting publicly. Today, though, they remain good friends.

Suddenly Single

At the moment, Carson is a single fella. Even though he's surrounded by talented women, and his adoring fans, he just hasn't found the right person yet. The girls he meets are generally from the entertainment industry and although Carson judges someone for who she is, rather than what she does, he has hinted he might not end up with a showbiz sweetheart. "I'm finding they're not the girls I'm attracted to philosophically," he told a reporter. "I want someone who has a sense of reality."

CHAPTER NINE
Cool Carson
Concepts

Name: Carson Daly
Middle name: Jones
Birthday: June 22, 1973
Born: Santa Monica, California
Current residence: Upper West Side in New York City
Family: Mom, Pattie; Stepdad, Richard; older Sister, Quinn; a dog and a cat
Hair color: Dark brown
Eye color: Blue
Height: 6'2"
Shoe size: 11½
Hobbies: playing golf video games
Sports activities: Golf, golf, golf
Least favorite thing to do: Fly
Nicest person interviewed: Jennifer Love Hewitt

Order of Events:

1991   Carson graduates from Santa Monica High School then attends one semester at Loyola Marymount University studying theology.

1992   Carson transfers to a college in Palm Springs, now considering a life-time career in golf.

1993   Carson starts interning at KCMJ, a radio station in Palm Springs.

1994   Carson starts moonlighting at another radio station 100 miles away while still working at KCMJ. He then makes a move to 105 FM.

1995-96 Carson snags a cool job at KOME. He works there for a bit, then gets a great gig at KROQ and starts to get noticed by lots of people in the music industry.

1997   MTV offers Carson a three month gig hosting the summer show *Beach House*. After that, he makes the leap to another MTV show, *Motel California*.

1998   This is a big year for Carson. MTV gives him the chance to do live TV. He and a few other hosts helm in a show called *MTV Live*. In September, *MTV Live* merges with *Total Request*. Carson becomes the host of this new show now called *Total Request Live*. He also meets Jennifer Love Hewitt when he interviews her. They start dating. Carson becomes a household name.

1999 Carson's fame train is running at top speed. He is voted by *Teen* magazine as the *Coolest MTV Guy* and *TRL* wins the *Can't Miss TV Show* category. Carson is an introducer at both the *Video Music Awards*, and at the *WB Radio Music Awards*. The show is taped live from one of his favorite places, Las Vegas, where he introduces Garth Brooks. Carson also starts making lots of TV appearances on talk shows like *The Donnie and Marie Show*, *Politically Incorrect*, *The Tonight Show with Jay Leno*, *The Regis & Kathie Lee Show*, and hosts the *Miss Teen USA Pageant*. He also is interviewed in tons of magazines including: *Teen People*,

Teen Celebrity, Newsweek, Entertainment Weekly, People, Teen, Seventeen, Twist, Popstar, J-14, and *YM.* Alas, 1999 is an unhappy year love wise. In October, Carson and Jennifer split. By November, though, Carson bounces back when he is named the Sexiest Broadcaster by *People.*

2000 Carson hosts *MTV's New Year's Eve Millennium Blast,* MTV's *Super Bowl Party,* and the *Miss USA Pageant.* In March, he became a columnist for *US* magazine and commentator on TV's *Entertainment Tonight.* He stars in two commercials, and has a cameo in MTV's *2gether* made-for-TV-movie.

Carson's Horoscope

Birthday: June 22
Sign: Cancer
Symbol: Crab
Element: Water
Best day of the week: Monday
Color: Light blue and silver

Gem: Moonstone and pearl, which are associated with good fortune and harmony
Ruling Planet: The moon
Lucky numbers: 3 and 7

Even though Carson is technically on the cusp of Gemini and Cancer, Carson proclaims, "I think I'm a Cancer because I'm one of those sensitive types," he told *J-14*. Still, he likes to read *both* horoscopes and often picks the better of the two!

Cancers are loyal people, and that's his best quality. When Carson says he's going to do something, he comes through. He never breaks a promise, and hardly ever lets a friend down. Cancers are supportive, sympathetic, and always ready to lend a helping hand or give a friend or co-worker encouragement.

Carson's symbol, the Crab, suggests a hard-core exterior with a soft side underneath. Carson is a sensitive fella with good morals. He's far more interested in helping people than becoming a mega star or even using his star status for self promotion.

Most important to Cancers are food, home — and sleep! They love to eat, and you can bet their refrigerators are filled with all sorts of goodies. In Carson's case, you'll find frozen pizza, Slim Jims, Otter Pops, and cheese, cheese, cheese.

Though they can be stubborn and childlike, they are good at easing tension and possess fine leadership qualities. Sounds like the job of a host.

Cancers are protective and care deeply about family members and close friends. Just look at how close Carson is with his mom, stepdad, and sister.

In a recent article in *Twist* magazine, Carson's handwriting was analyzed. It revealed our hottie host has a great sense of responsibility toward the people around him — there's that loyalty thing — and that sometimes, he can feel like a loner — there's that Crab exterior.

Part of Carson's charm is his modest, shy quality. He also has a good sense of humor, and a beautiful smile. He's quick and snappy with comments while being sarcastic and charming at the same time. His dry sense of humor, Cheshire cat grin, and deadpan facial expressions sometimes make it hard for fans to know when he's teasing and kidding around. But that's all part of his allure. He really *is* the guy next door. Everyone wants to be his friend.

Awards

For the past two years *Teen* magazine honored Carson with the Favorite MTV VJ award. Modest Carson was bowled over, but perhaps what was most shocking to the humble host was when *People* named him Sexiest Broadcaster. Carson was stunned. "I didn't believe it when they called," and he told Regis and Kathie Lee on their show. Still, he thought someone was trying to pull the wool over his eyes — and that person was his mom. He called her immediately, asking her what she had done, but Pattie was innocent.

CHAPTER TEN
Private
Daly

So, you think you know all about Carson from watching *TRL* and reading every magazine profile? Think again. There is more to this superstar than meets the press's eye. He may be a celebrity in public, but in private, he is just a regular guy.

Carson's Teenage Years

We all had courses in high school that we didn't exactly love, and Carson is no exception. While he owned honors English (his favorite book was *Heart of Darkness*) and history, math and science were not his strong suits. As a matter of fact, when he opened his first checking account he took his mother with him to help out, and his sister used to do his taxes for him. By having other people help him, Carson avoided making mistakes. Which is not so easy to do in science class. When mathematical equations became more important than Bunsen burners, Carson decided that he was not destined to be a scientist.

Outside class Carson was a typical teenager in every way. He loved music and by the time he was a junior in high school tunes had become a huge part of his life. His musical interests and influences were vast and varied; for each different situation he had corresponding music. Alone, he liked to listen to all Top 40. But when he and his friends were hanging out in Malibu, he grooved to such reggae bands as Bob Marley, Ziggy Marley, and Steel Pulse. And with his basketball buddies he was into N.W.A, Houdini, and many other rap groups. At home, the influence was a little different. When Carson's parents cooked dinner they put on such legends as the Eagles and James Taylor, hence, he also grew to love classic rock.

As a student in junior high and high school, Carson did not have the jaunty self-confidence that seems so natural to him on *TRL*. Growing up he was not a guy who liked to take risks — and he never got into trouble. The impact of his father's death caused him to be shy, introverted, and non-confrontational; it was not even until junior high that Carson truly dealt with the loss of his father at all. At that adolescent age Carson began to question why and how the universe could have allowed something so tragic to happen. Because his family has always been a huge source of strength and love for him, Carson relied upon his mother and stepfather's support while he struggled to make peace with his father's absence. Eventually, he developed a great religious faith that continues to sustain him today, and is partially responsible for his self-assurance and confidence.

With such a strong sense of himself, Carson does not let people ruffle him, no matter how much he is provoked. For example, sometimes he goes to watch Monday night football at a restaurant near his apartment and actually gets heckled by other patrons, guys who want to pick a fight with him because of his fame. Rather than react, however, Carson lets every insult roll right past him, a trick he says he developed in his sophomore year of high school when he decided to be an individualist rather than bow to peer pressures.

Carson doesn't mind standing alone for his principles, that's his personality. But he's also aware that in doing so, he can set a great example for the millions of young kids who are his fans. While he doesn't like to use *TRL* or his media exposure as a place to preach, Carson does feel extremely responsible for giving fans the right amount of advice and support they need. As often as he can, Carson takes a personal interest in the fans who write to him with problems. Sometimes, he even responds via telephone to try to help with a tricky situation.

"Because of my MTV exposure, I've had viewers reach out to me. One thirteen-year-old wrote to me about how her brother beats on her," he confided to *Teen People*. "I figured she probably hadn't let her parents in on this, but she was telling me, so I called her. We talked it over, and I tried to explain the difference between roughhousing and real abuse. In the end, I convinced her to tell her parents in a firm way that would make them listen. Her brother doesn't lay a hand on her now."

That caring, helpful attitude goes for his friends too, not just his fans. If Carson notices a friend behaving in a self-destructive way, making choices about anything that could have a negative impact, he's not shy about saying something. He likes to stop problems before they grow too large, so he'll speak to friends directly about worrisome behavior, or approach their parents for help rather than wait for disastrous consequences.

The Real Deal

Who is Carson really, now that he is all grown up and has embarked upon a mega-career that does not look like it will slow down any time soon? You guessed it, a very down to earth kind of guy. The kind who goes to church every Sunday (to give thanks for being so blessed with such a great career), gets nervous when he starts a new job (when he first started *TRL* everything was so new it took a while for him to build up his confidence), and suffers through romantic heartache the way the rest of us do (by using music as medicine, of course. Limp Bizkit's album, *Significant Other*, nursed him through a breakup last year). Despite all his fame Carson does not have a huge ego and remains a man devoted to being his true self.

It is clear to see that the true self is more than just a pretty face. Carson is a man of ideas, smarts and philosophies, too. For example, he believes music is not something to be dissected. For Carson, his response to any band, despite genre or style, is immediate and emotional; he hears a song and either responds to it or doesn't based on how easily he can relate to the lyrics and tune. When considering the current musical terrain, he predicts that there will be a return to rock as the cycle evolves from the grunge/alternative fad of the early 90s, through the explosion of feel-good pop music toward the end of the century, and now moves into a new phase where Testosterone Rock (as the new style has been dubbed) is becoming the latest fad.

Carson's future goals, however, do not hinge on his face always being in front of the camera; he has a large interest in creating the entertainment, rather than being it. Making good, quality television and film have become increasingly important to him. These days, he spends all of his free time (Usually on an airplane!) studying film production. The idea of producing, writing and directing film's is a growing interest to him. During the shoot for a Super Bowl commercial earlier this year he spent most of the fourteen-hour day asking the director questions so that he could learn about the craft.

But what else would Carson be doing with his life if, shudder to think, he *wasn't* hosting *TRL*? Becoming a priest isn't really an option anymore. Golf is still a relaxing hobby, but also no longer a career goal. Carson is under contract to *TRL*, but he may be looking to branch out. He could go into consulting — for the past year, TV networks have been sending the star scripts for upcoming shows asking Carson if teens will like them or not.

Lately, he's been hanging with the film folks at MTV. Since Carson wants to try his hand at directing, producing, and writing movies, MTV is certainly the right place for him to break into these different arenas. He and Jason have written a script together and you can be sure they'd probably love to see it filmed — and with Jason's production and directing credits it's not an impossible goal to reach. The script, based loosely around their own lives, is about two guys living in the city, hanging out and getting into trouble here and there — wackiness ensues. And now that other doors are opening for him, Carson is receptive to the idea of acting as well.

Carson has one other "hidden" desire. It's no secret he loves music. It wouldn't be surprising to see him produce an album. He recently joined forces with friend and lead singer of Smash Mouth, Steve Harwell. Together, they started Spunout Records. Fans have even seen him with a guitar — a dangerous object for a music buff. "It's a hidden passion of mine," he admitted to MTV on-line. "[But] no, you will never ever, ever have to *hear* it."

Perhaps journalism is his next quest. Recently, he's started doing some columns for *US* magazine. He's also been offered a semi-permanent segment on *Entertainment Tonight* called *Conversations With Carson.*

Does all this self-imposed responsibility get overwhelming? You bet it does! But Carson wants to help everyone as much as possible. He often accomplishes this by sacrificing his privacy as he lets his fans know him personally. To him, this sacrifice is part of his spiritual ethic; he didn't become a priest, but the principles of religion and giving play a large role in his day to day life. Doing a good job, caring about his work and about the kids who watch the show is crucial to Carson.

"I think it's a new style of religion in a way. It's more a 'good person' philosophy than a hard-core religious fanaticism." Maybe all things *do* happen for a reason and that we're *led* down specific paths, rather than making choices. At least it seems that way for Carson. He's become a positive role model, and reaches tons more teens on TV than if he had become a priest.

"As a priest I might have touched a few hundred people; at MTV I have potential to reach so many more. God's put me here for a reason. This is where I need to be."

Carson's story wouldn't be complete without a little advice from our hero.

"Watch MTV, but listen to your parents," he told *Newsday*. "All the stuff you see on TV, like *Spring Break* and in the movies, is made out to be really super cool, and stuff you should be doing. Well, *I* never did that. Enjoy what you see in the media but don't feel that's what you have to do. Your parents may seem really stupid now, but believe me, they get smart real quick." Most important, Carson wants to send a positive message out to his fans. "If I can help in some way — not to be preachy, but there are a lot of kids who need someone to talk to and I'm accessible."

Carson has also become a voice for his generation. "I think there's a large part of our generation that really have their act together," he explained to Regis and Kathie Lee. "You know, appreciate their jobs, appreciate their parents, appreciate their lives. Especially if they're young and making it." Who could ask for a better spokesperson?

CHAPTER ELEVEN
Fan
Fair

Some say one's success stems from
talent, others claim it's who you know —
connections — not what you know or how
good you are at your job. Then there are
the believers who insist it's a combination
of both. Truth be told, most of Carson's
success came from his great personality,
nice-guy appeal and level-headedness.
Plus, he's a great interviewer. But fans
play a huge part in Carson's life, too.

Carson is a true rarity. Not only is
he committed to his work, but he thor-
oughly takes his viewers into consideration. That's not something all stars do. In
fact, it's still hard for him to admit he's a
star. "I'm not convinced it's me you love,"
he told a loyal viewer during an on-line

chat, who asked him what it's like to be loved by so many fans. "But more, the incredibly handsome and talented boy bands I deliver to your homes every day. Let's not get the two confused. But thanks for the compliment."

He also calls fans who have written to him. He always takes the time to sign an autograph, pose for a photo, or just hang out with fans and chat. "When I walk out of work and all those kids are there, it's like there's two hundred of my friends," he told the *New York Post*. Now that's sweet.

Street Interviews

Devoted fans who have traveled far and wide come from all over the world just to get a chance to see the "master" at work. They stand for hours trying to be seen, holding up posters and signs, screaming their lungs out — all to snag a glimpse from the host. Some, who are eighteen or older, are invited upstairs into the magic kingdom where they get a first hand view of Carson, and the special, often surprising guests that appear on the show. Some hope to grab their own fifteen minutes of fame. As the microphone gets passed around, audience members say a quick hello, introduce their video, and say why they requested it. Many other fans must endure the wait outside, often standing on line or in a circle surrounding the MTV building. These loyal viewers can only see their main man through the huge glass windows. Here are Carson comments from these dedicated fans:

1. "He's hot and has a great smile and he's really innocent looking. The show is great 'cause it's not just random videos, it's videos that everybody likes so they're going to be really good. I like when they bring in guest stars like Puff Daddy, Britney Spears, and Christina Aguilera." Katie, 12

2. "The part I like best about *TRL* is Carson and that's the only reason I watch. He's really cute and always makes jokes and stuff. I would want to go someplace with him where I could talk to him and get to know him." Amy, 16

3. "Carson is nice and funny and the show is about youth and having fun. He

acts like he enjoys his job. He's cute and he knows his stuff. He lets you know what kind of music he likes when he introduces the songs, so he's kind of telling you a little bit about himself." Anna, 16

4. "My favorite part is that you can call in. My friend called in for Korn, she also got on the show. She got to meet Carson and said he was really nice." Megan, 14

5. "Carson was doing *TRL* with the audience outside and he was totally cool with everybody. He came outside and went up and talked to everybody. Afterwards he was signing autographs and he seemed like a regular guy and down to earth." Geron, 18

6. "He brings a lot of cool people on the show. He's like one of the teenagers, and he's not considered an older guy. He's hip. He has nice eyes and hair." Jasman, 15

7. "I like everything about him. He makes the show enjoyable. I watch *TRL* every day and it's changed my music tastes. I didn't like Kid Rock and since I saw him on the

countdown I've started to like him."
Denise, 15

8. "I can request a video and see what *I* want, not what they choose." Sammy, 14

9. "Carson knows that we love him. He's really cool and he does a great job. We can see what's happening through the window, and that's really cool." Shanna, 14

10. "I've been here since seven in the morning. My feet are so frostbitten. There are seven of us here. This is dedicated. Carson is down to earth and really cool and we get to see 'N Sync, so it's worth it." Amanda, 15

11. "I like the show. We decided to come here and dance, even if it's outside." Rudy, 15

12. "He's a guy who's really down to earth and talks about real issues and people's problems. He's a cool guy. If we could spend the day together I'd love to go to the movies and have dinner with him." Jennifer, 15

13. "I've been waiting for five hours. Just to get a glimpse of him is worth it. He's so hot and he has a great attitude. I'd love to find out why he broke up with Jennifer Love Hewitt." Jane, 14

14. "He's got good looks and he's gorgeous all the way around. It's cool to see all the groups come down and it's fun when the celebrities call up and see what they like." Tara, 13

15. "Carson is normal and happy. *TRL* is special because it's live and spontaneous, and entertaining and you can see what's happening. It's young and fun." Arleen, 18

16. "He's cute and he's sweet. I've been here since this morning. We drove forty-five minutes away just to be here and see him." Dominique, 16

17. "I like *TRL* because of the guests and the variety of music they play. I love Carson's eyes, his sense of humor, his sarcastic personality. If I could spend the day with him, we'd go ice skating and then

take a horse and buggy ride around Central Park." Gretchen, 17

18. "I like Carson because he seems like a really down to earth guy. He's out there doing his job. I see him go to all these high-class events and he's always saying 'I'm glad they let a scruffy guy like me in the place.' I came all the way from Hawaii, a 12 hour flight, just to see him and be in New York." Audra, 27

19. "I'm a big fan. I watch the show every day. And I'd stand out here all day, no matter how long it takes just to get him to see us. Carson is cool. He's just so cute." Jarin, 26

20. "Carson has great looks and beautiful eyes. He's such a great host. He always knows just what to say. And he picks people out of the crowd to be in the audience and I think that's just so kind." Maria, 16

21. "He's a really nice guy. He's awesome and so cute. I love the fact that the show is

live, that you get to request what videos you
like. It's a really teenage show." Angeline, 17

22. "He's great. He's natural and fun. His
whole face is just gorgeous. If I could
spend the day with him, I'd hang out and
go to the mall, maybe we'd go shopping.
He's so real and alive. There's nothing fake
about him." Michele, 14

23. "One of the reasons I came to New York
was to see *TRL* because I watch it all the
time. I think Carson is really funny. The
show is really hard to do, and he does it
everyday." Amy, 15,

24. "He's hot and funny. The guests are
great and the videos are cool. It's an awesome show because it's what everyone
voted for that day." Tiffany, 14

25. "He seems like a nice guy. He's single —
and ready to mingle. Because the show is
live, anything can happen, like the Backstreet Boys could get kicked off the countdown. Moments can just happen." Gillian,
14

arson. I love him so much. He's
...t and fun to watch. Even though there
are celebrity guests, it's still nice to come
back and see Carson. He keeps the show
interesting. He holds your attention. People call up and say they love him and he's
really modest about that." Janelle, 16

27. "I met him once, and he was really nice
to talk to, really down to earth. I was just
there and everyone else was going crazy
and we were talking. I think he really appreciated the fact I wasn't freaking out or
worshipping the ground he walked on. I
watch the show every day and love the fact
that it's live." Trisha, 16

28. "I think Carson is a cutie and that the
show is different everyday. His personality
seems great and he has a great smile. I like
hearing about his mom. It's cute. It's nice
that he had a good relationship with his
mom." Jennifer, 20

CHAPTER TWELVE
Total
Trivia

Total Carson fans shouldn't have any trouble answering these questions. But in case you need a little help, you can find the answers at the end.

1. Where is Carson most ticklish?

   A. feet
   B. waist
   C. neck
   D. stomach

2. What does he hate?

   A. small spaces
   B. driving
   C. flying
   D. the boogey man

3. In order to celebrate the 100th episode of *MTV Live*, what special group did Carson play?

    A. Smash Mouth
    B. Korn
    C. Backstreet Boys
    D. LFO

Bonus: What was the song?
    A. ". . . Baby One More Time"
    B. "Smooth"
    C. "I Do"
    D. "Why Can't We Be Friends"

4. Which nails does Carson paint?

    A. first and third fingers
    B. last two fingers
    C. third and fourth fingers
    D. first two fingers

Bonus: what color?
    A. black
    B. red
    C. pink
    D. brown

5. What celebrity does Carson most re-member meeting at the 1997 *MTV Video Music Awards*?

   A. Alanis Morissette
   B. Mike Tyson
   C. Jewel
   D. Adrian Young

6. Who was Carson's prom date?

   A. his girlfriend
   B. his mother
   C. his stepmother
   D. his sister

Bonus: What did they do?

   A. went dancing
   B. went bowling
   C. nothing
   D. watched television

7. What singer creates a little "mood music" for Carson?

A. Brian McKnight
B. Barbra Streisand
C. Britney Spears
D. Michael Bolton

8. Who did Carson introduce at the WB Radio Music Awards?

A. Lenny Kravitz
B. Christina Aguilera
C. Garth Brooks
D. Mariah Carey

9. What does Carson use as coasters?

   A. napkins
   B. books
   C. old records
   D. CDs

Bonus: Which is his favorite artist to use?

   A. Pink Floyd
   B. Michael Jackson
   C. Phil Collins
   D. Elton John

10. What body part did Carson break while skiing?

    A. leg
    B. back
    C. arm
    D. neck

Bonus: Which sibling team took over as hosts for him on Live MTV till he was better?

   A. Donnie and Marie Osmond
   B. Janet and Michael Jackson
   C. Alex and Eddie Van Halen
   D. Ahmet and Dweezil Zappa

Multiple choice answers:

1. B
2. C
3. A

bonus: D

4. B

bonus: A

5. B
6. C

bonus: D

7. A
8. C
9. D

bonus: B

10. B

bonus: D

Test more of your knowledge with these true/false questions.

1. Carson eats a Hershey chocolate bar every day.

2. Carson wears contacts.

3. Carson only plays the songs on TRL he likes.

4. Carson had his nose pierced when he was younger.

5. Carson was the first DJ to play Smash Mouth.

6. Before each show, Carson sings a Korn song.

7. Carson and Jason have two dogs.

8. Carson's mom calls him Carsy Cakes.

9. Carson once caddied for O.J. Simpson.

10. If Carson had a son, he'd name him Jack.

11. The first 'N Sync video Carson played was "Tearin' Up My Heart."

12. Carson has a secret crush on Britney Spears.

13. Carson's favorite Third Eye Blind song is "London."

14. Carson would like to appear on the cover of Time.

15. TRL has played over 350 videos.

16. Before sharing an apartment with Jason, Carson shared an apartment with Fred Durst.

17. Carson once considered becoming a professional surfer.

18. Carson drinks soda before he goes on the air.

19. Carson has square danced with Hanson on TV.

20. Carson's favorite Madonna movie is Desperately Seeking Susan.

21. Carson's favorite MTV VJ was Martha Quinn.

True/False answers:

1. F	12. F
2. T	13. T
3. T	14. T
4. T	15. F
5. T	16. F
6. F	17. F
7. F	18. T
8. T	19. T
9. T	20. T
10. T	21. T
11. T	

More Private Daly Facts

1. Favorite color: Blue
2. Favorite teams: LA Lakers, Oakland Raiders, and Notre Dame's Fighting Irish
3. Favorite book: The Bible
4. Favorite movies: *Barfly* and *Willy Wonka*
5. Favorite actress: Faye Dunaway
6. Favorite actor: Michael Rappaport
7. Favorite Marcy Playground song: "St. Joe on the School Bus"
8. Favorite musicians: Smash Mouth, Nine Inch Nails, Third Eye Blind, Blink 182, Less Than Jake, Beastie Boys, Kid Rock. Oh so many . . .
9. Favorite food: Pizza, Slim Jims and Otter Pops
10. Favorite clothing designers: Are you kidding? This guys loves jeans and T-shirts
11. Favorite TV show? *Politically Incorrect With Bill Maher*

CHAPTER THIRTEEN
Get
in Touch

Internet sites are great places for finding out additional information on Carson. Here are two fabulous ones. They have great facts, hard-to-find information, past articles, quotes, personal stories and more.

1. www.mtvpages.com/users/TRL/

If you like MTV, you'll love this site. It's an absolute *TRL* gold mine. Find out which artists have made it to the top ten, take a quiz, or read up on the *TRL* staff. Click onto "My *TRL* Experience" to read letters from teens who have met Carson, or get bios on Carson, Ananda Lewis, and Dave Holmes. You can also get information about various artists who have appeared on the show. On your way out, sign the guest book or read what past fans have written.

2. www.carsondaly.com/index.html

The "Approved Carson Daly Page" is the most in-depth Carson site. Almost every article, interview, on-line chat or TV appearance Carson has given can be found here, along with news updates, a mailing list, fan stuff, scrapbook, bio, quotes, and additional links. Read up on Pattie, Jason, and a list of Carson's favorite things. Creators Lyndsay, Dani, Amy, and Jessica are the masterminds behind this incredible site. Kudos to them.

Got something you'd like to say to Carson? Don't feel like surfing the web? A handwritten note is a always cool. Here's how to contact him.

Carson Daly
c/o: MTV Viewer Services
1515 Broadway
New York, NY 10036